PIANO ACCOMPANIMENT

Solo Pieces

for the

Intermediate Clarinetist

(With Piano Accompaniment)

By Dr. Norman Heim

Visit us on the Web at www.melbay.com — E-mail us at email@melbay.com

Contents

1. Presto from Suite

G.F.Telemann
(1681–1767)

Fine

4

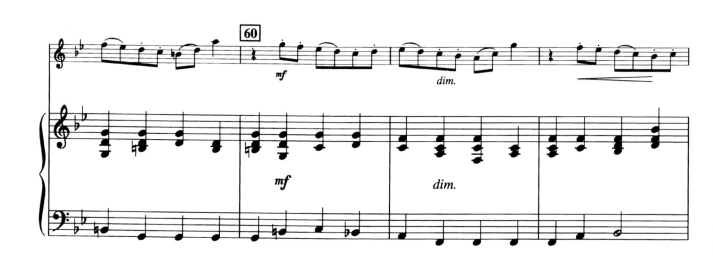

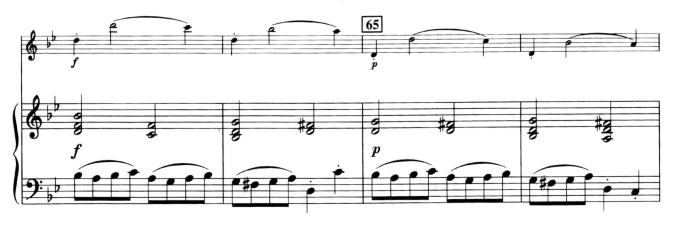

D.C. el Fine

2. Voluntary

Jeremiah Clark
(1673–1707)

3. Three Movements from French Suite
a. Sarabande

J.S. Bach
(1685–1750)

b. Minuet

15

c. Gavotte

4. Le Tambourin

Jean Phillipe Rameau
(1683–1764)

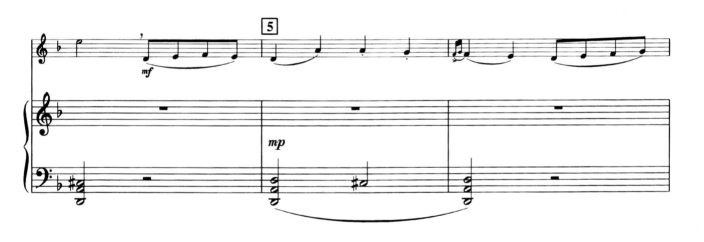

19

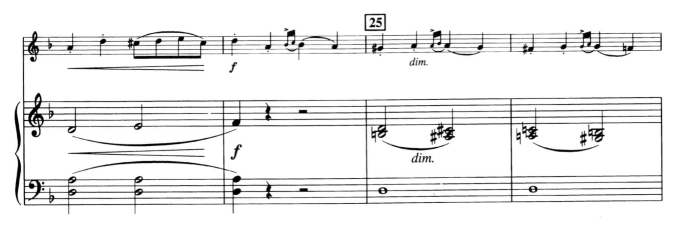

5. Minuet, Sarabande and Courrente

a. Minuet

G.F.Handel
(1685–1759)

b. Sarabande

27

Variation 2

c. Courrente

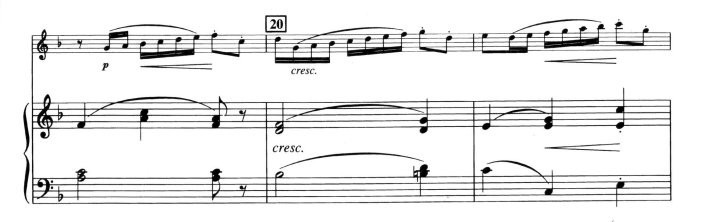

6. Finale from Sonata

Franz Josef Haydn
(1732–1809)

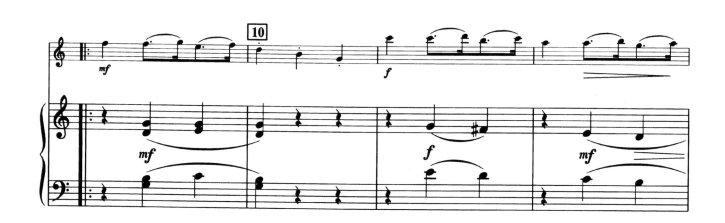

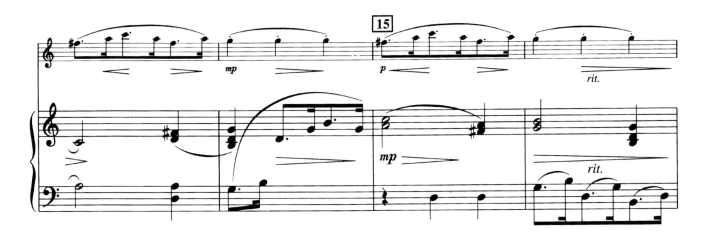

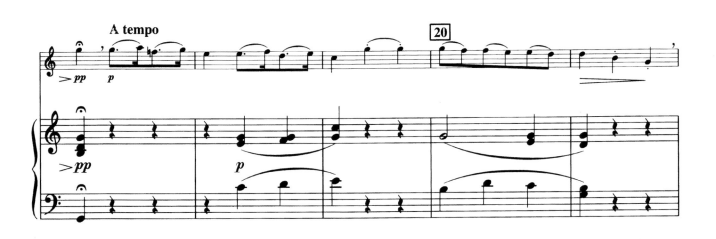

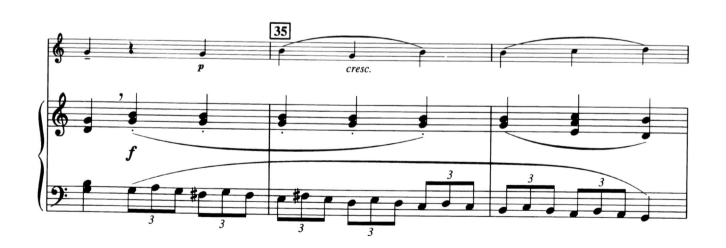

7. Minuet

Luigi Boccherini
(1743–1805)

41

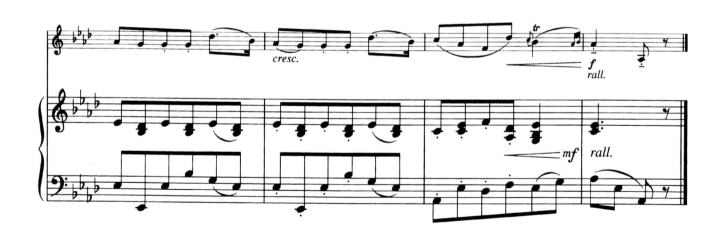

8. Allegro from Sonatina

Wolfgang A. Mozart
(1756–1791)

47

52

9. Largo from Sonata in B-flat

Ludwig von Beethoven
(1770–1827)

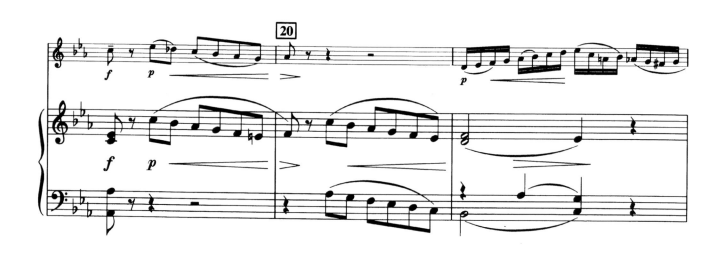

10. Sonata No. 2, Op. 65 - Allegro Maestoso e Vivace

Felix Mendelssohn
(1809–1847)

58

59

11. Menuetto

Franz Schubert
(1797–1828)

Fine

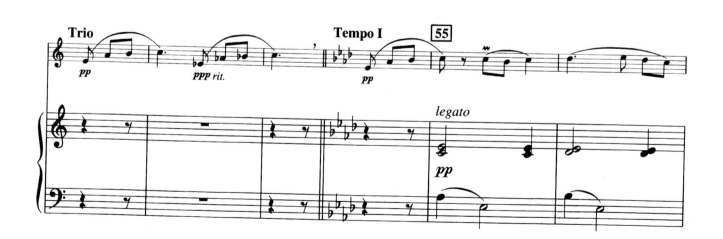

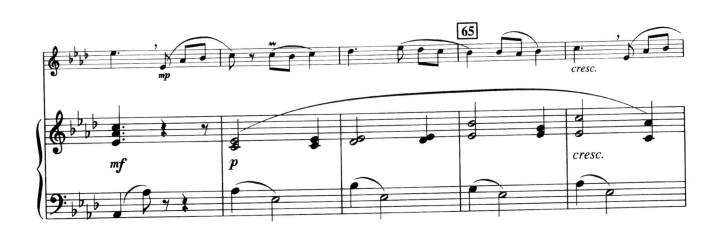

12. Intermezzo Op. 118, No. 2

Johannes Brahms
(1833–1897)

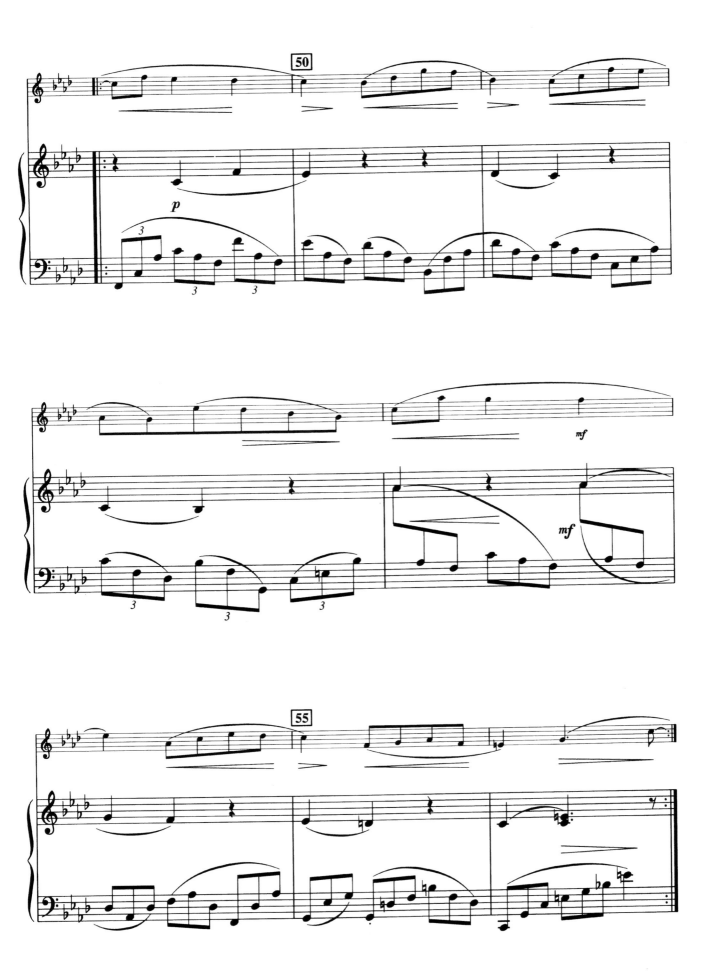

75

13. Vocalise Op. 34, No.14

Sergei Rachmaninoff
(1873–1943)

20 **Poco piu mosso**

25

14. Told at Sunset from Suite Op. 51

Edward Mac Dowell
(1860–1908)

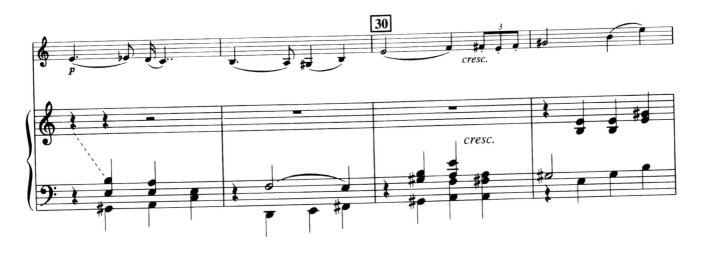

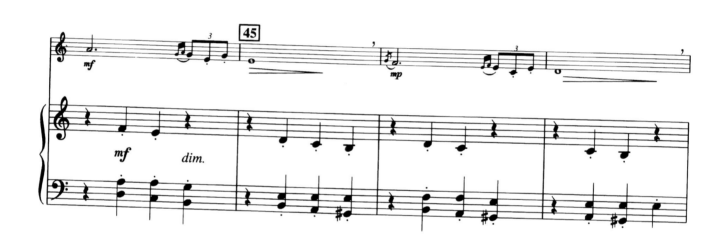

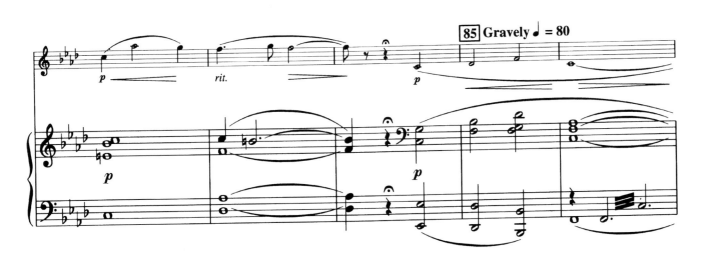

15. Berceuse Op. 16

Gabriel Fauré
(1845–1924)

94

95